S0-BUB-403

TO **SELF** BE TRUE

The Search Within

"From harmony, from heavenly harmony,
The universal frame began:
When nature underneath a heap
Of jarring atoms lay,
And could not heave her head,
The tuneful voice was heard from high,
'Arise ye more than dead!'
Then cold, and hot, and moist and dry,
In order to their stations leap,
And music's power obey,
From harmony, from heavenly harmony,
This universal frame began:
From harmony to harmony
Through all the compass of the notes it ran,
The diapason closing full in man."

John Dryden

"*The Aquarian Age is approaching the phase of manifestation. The time has come when the spiritual desire to serve the Creator is rising within the consciousness of humanity and the energy generated by that desire is growing beyond the comprehension of mankind. It will become the controlling force upon the earth in spite of the great unrest and the predictions of wars among the nations. As the desire to serve is increased or multiplied, peace surpassing the accepted nature of peace will descend upon all. As you continue to desire to serve your Creator, you generate the power to avert war and to promote this peace.*"

Lessons for the Aquarian Age (to be published)

TO **SELF** BE TRUE

The Search Within

Received by Amy Loomis;
Compiled and edited by
Evarts Loomis

Friendly Hills Fellowship, Publisher
26126 Fairview Ave.
Hemet, California 92344

©Copyright 1991 by Friendly Hills Fellowship.
ISBN #0-9630266-0-7

The material in this book must not be reproduced in part or as a whole without written permission from the compiler and editor.

Contents

PART ONE: THE PERSONAL SELF

1. THE INDIVIDUAL (the Ego)

2. SOLVING HUMAN PROBLEMS

3. THE BODY TEMPLE

4. SPIRITUAL VALUES

5. SPIRITUAL PROGRESS

Contents vii

8. FROM THE SPIRITUAL TO THE COSMIC

PART TWO: THE IMPERSONAL SELF

9. FROM THE self TO THE SELF

10. THE COSMIC STATE

11. LIGHTING THE WAY

Acknowledgements

My heart-felt thanks go out first to Rev. Lolita Hughes and John Chitty for their invaluable corrections and editing skills, to Katherine Smith for help designing the cover; and to Karla Brandt for her painting entitled "In the beginning" done while listening to the music of Haydn's Creation.

Introduction

The following material came through to Amy Loomis between the years 1956 and 1964. In all she typed out, as she was directed to do, about 2000 pages as a labor of love. They were not only an instrument for her own spiritual illumination and attainment but for many others who came to know her. These pages together with authentic instruction from others closely related to the same Higher Source, are shared in the hope that those who read and linger to study will choose to apply them in the best way suited to their own soul evolvement, and the purpose of the Great Ones who watch over and guide us.

I, the editor and compiler of this material, have the privilege of having been Amy's son and fellow traveler in our search for life's meaning over a period of many years.

As she would have said, "The object of all spiritual work is to consciously experience the Presence of God, thus convincing yourself beyond all doubt that God Is All There Is."

As eloquently expressed in the following messages, God Is Infinite Love— pulsation to be felt as a flame in the heart; and as Peace— the product of Love and Light.

E.G.L

Chapter 1

THE INDIVIDUAL, or EGO

God and Man

The meaning of creation is that God thought of separate expressions of Himself and they became manifest as the separate and complete expressions that are known as man, beast, vegetable and mineral kingdoms.

Realize that you are but a thought of God and as such are functioning as a mental being, temporarily clothed in flesh and bone in order to function in this world.

Know, too, that the nature of the will or desire is the manifestation of the individual personality, and that the will or desire expressed by individuals is the difference between them.

Some will desire to serve God, others mammon. The decision is that of the individual.

The reason for this choice is that the individual must of himself seek God before he can begin to express as God intended him to be.

The Soul

The soul is not only the counterpart of spirit, but the spirit within the center of not only physical and spiritual beings, but of the Cosmic Being which exists outside of or beyond the physical and spiritual components. Cosmic Being comprises the entire grouping of separate atoms or particles of substance attested to be God's substance, though differentiated to produce the necessary phenomena of physical and spiritual expressions of existence.

The Personal Will

The will of the individual is all that he possesses in his own right. Everything else belongs to God.

Individuals function in their own right until such time as the desire to express selfishly is relinquished to the Source from whence it came.

There will of necessity be times when the personal will becomes so closely bound with the impersonal that you are to wonder how you reached the decisions confronting you with so little reasoning or effort of your conscious mind.

Surrender of the personal will is the point of initiation of true desire[1] to serve God, which eventually leads to flooding the subconscious mind with spiritual power.

The Will to Live

The will to serve God is the link between the spiritual plane and earth. Thought is the key which opens the switch, turns on the power, and places one within the very radiance of God.

When the will to live is strong, the power is like a fountain of energy which flows until the individual ceases to will it to flow.

The individual ceases to desire to struggle as the physical body begins to loosen its hold. A confused mental state makes it difficult to coordinate the spiritual and physical states. At this point one loses the power to retain the spiritual attributes within the physical frame and disassociates from the physical shell. The mental and spiritual attributes become merged, leaving the shell of the physical organism to gradually cease to function.

The Personality (the Ego)

The soul builds the personality for the purpose of growth and development. Personality is first cultivated and used as a tool for service. It is later discarded on the journey back to the Source from whence we came.

While expressing as personality here on earth, you tend to forget the Source of your being. You become engrossed in the world of the personality and delay your return. You become imprisoned in your human concerns.

As a person becomes aware of God as the Source of his being, he begins to live from that Center. The desire to impress others through the personality begins to disappear from consciousness, leaving only the relationship between God and His creation.

Personality is a limited and self-centered expression of being, and as such is unaware of service to God. As the personality is infused with the Will of God, and led to service, it can be trained to serve My Will.

Be of cheerful heart. As you continue to desire to serve Me you will increase your vibration rate, and will be used to carry out My Will.

Physical Beauty

Both worldly beauty and power count as naught in spiritual development, rendering the possessor vulnerable to temptations of the flesh or material nature, thus retarding spiritual growth.

Mind

The conscious mind can actually destroy physical bodily functioning   unless spiritual power or awareness is established and becomes a vibrating force within one's being.

The quiet mind imbued with spirit is like a breath of peaceful desire born in the heart.

Thought

The power of thought is the most powerful of all vibrations emitted from human beings. Humanity as an expression of the soul is conscious, and the strongest vibrations coming from the consciousness are thoughts.

Thought acts as the initiator of any action, emotionally or physically possible within the individual. Because it sets things in motion, it is the key to open the switch which controls the circuit of vibration and thus determines all effects.

Be mindful of your thoughts. Spiritual thoughts create spiritual energy and activity, and result in positive effects. Negative or selfish thoughts generate barriers which impede spiritual power.

Consciousness impulses the mind with desire. The mind registers impressions and directs these impulses according to the individual's state of awareness. A receptive mind will take the Truth as expressed and using the heart as the instrument of purification, will send the truth out through the emotion of love.

All thoughts are known to God, because they originate in God. The way you receive these mental impulses and how you express them individually, is noted; for it is through these experiences that you are trained. Nothing is hidden from God.

Be aware of the quality of your thoughts, whether they be trivial, harmless, or selfish. You will be faced consciously with choices. Some thoughts you will want to surrender and merge with God's consciousness. Other thoughts will cause concern, and they will need to be released and replaced.

There are myriad possibilities for each recorded thought or desire to be erased as they are released into the lighter atmosphere of consciousness. As an individual progresses on the journey back to God, he becomes increasingly aware of Cosmic Energy that fills all space beyond even space as we know it. As one continues to live in accordance with his higher understanding of God's law, he will refine and direct his thoughts to ever higher purposes.

Everything begins in consciousness, therefore the

vibration of thought exceeds all others. Your work is to bring all thoughts into alignment with God's purpose as they impact your mind.

As the ability to strengthen and purify your thoughts increases, a flame will be kindled within your body, so that you become a channel through which the Power of God surges. You will be able to bless all components of God's creation as you move through your day.

As you think in your heart, so will you express to those around you. Heed the thoughts that impulse your mind, and be mindful of the way you express them. Let them not register negatively against another person or situation. Remember that the one who holds the harmful thought will be the sufferer. If you find yourself entertaining harmful thoughts against another, will the power of love to flow through that person or situation.

Individual states of mind vary according to spiritual growth and development, therefore thoughts will be received in individual ways. The acceptance of an idea is an opportunity to:

Think of the spiritual power generated by God.

Include Me as a constituent which generates that power.

Purify the desire to serve God, and experience Cosmic Healing.

Since all ideas originate in Consciousness before they impact upon your mind, it is the purity of the idea that comprises its power.

The individual may have difficulty putting these ideas into words. Therefore words are not as important as the essence of the idea seeking expression.

The human mind is capable of expressing thoughts filled with venom, or filled with blessing, according to how he views his life situation. Therefore, human thoughts, carelessly scattered, can produce negative effects.

Consciousness is the link between the spiritual plane and the earth. In recognizing that all ideas begin in consciousness, the one who desires to serve God will use the thoughts impacting his mind to open the switch which allows the power to flow through him and place all within the radiance of God. This opportunity is available to all, but many are not yet aware of this.

You are being trained to recognize God as the Creator of the universe and all that is therein. This recognition initiates the selfless desire to serve, and generates the power to be utilized through you.

Thought, as the strongest vibration in the universe, when properly used, can produce results unmeasurable by human standards.

Thoughts, coming from a mind aligned with God, are like living embers, and have the power to ignite response from those toward whom they are directed. Thoughts have the power to generate physical changes within the body.

Be ever watchful of the words that you speak, or silently hold as opinions within your mind. One who is seeking your help is very vulnerable to the vibrations registering within the mind. As your mind is impacted with ideas from the Higher Self you are free to receive them and use them as you will; so is the seeker's mind impacted by what you say and believe. He will receive these thoughts in a way that he can understand and is very vulnerable to suggestions. Remember that at all times Love and Light can generate Peace.

The Intellect

The intellect is not to be trusted in spiritual matters because it is the result of human thinking.

Unless the human intellect is surrendered completely to God, it cannot be used as a vehicle of intelligent action.

Judge not the intellectual personality, who is
convinced of his knowledge of the way things work
on earth. Be ever ready to share the simplicity of
Love, Light, Power and Perfection of God. The
intellect has its place, but the simplicity of Love
through the Heart of God is the higher way.

Dreams

Dreams are not infallible, but are indicative of
states existing in the subconscious mind which reach
the surface and overflow, registering as visions or
experiences seemingly being physically enacted.

The Rhythm of Life

The rhythm of life is the universal rhythm and is a
component part of your being.

The rhythm of an individual varies with the spiritual
consciousness. As the spiritual consciousness is raised
from one level to a higher one, the rhythm becomes
attuned or corresponds.

Until the conscious mind decides to serve God, this
universal rhythm lies dormant, yet seems to be
expressed through physical patterns of expression
with which you are familiar.

The personality of the individual not only is governed by rhythm, but is controlled to such a degree that a forced change in the natural rhythm results in frustration and bewilderment that causes the individual to behave as a stranger to himself and those who know him.

Physical and spiritual rhythms are not the same. As the individual brings his thoughts into alignment with spiritual energy, he increasingly becomes an instrument for service to God. Then the personality rhythms are refined and brought into different rates of vibration.

The rhythm of life remains constant as it was at the time of birth. However, as the personality goes through various changes, the physical condition or nervous tension under which the individual functions may change with time and in tempo. In spite of temporary conditions, remember that the rhythm of life is the result of Cosmic Energy and remains undisturbed.

Rhythm is a result of Cosmic Energy generated through conscious desire to serve our Creator.

Blend with the rhythm. Accept it as a silent partner. As the spiritual consciousness is raised from one level to another, the rhythm will become attuned to this increased spirituality.

You are to realize that as a part of the substance of God, you came into being in the physical form with the universal rhythm already in play. Through the changes that take place in your personality, this rhythm remains the same, and you will be given opportunities to become more aware of its steady pace.

Vibration

The vibration of an individual remains constant, even though during the life span on earth, the frequency changes according to experiences of the personality.

Physical expression requires a lower rate of vibration than does the spiritual. The frequency rate can be altered in various ways, causing pain and physical symptoms that are not readily apparent in the body. As Cosmic Power permeates the body, sensations and nervous reactions to sudden circulatory changes may take place. The individual's ability to tolerate these chemical changes varies.

The act of reaching toward God will initiate transformation and an increased vibratory rate.

You are capable of channeling Cosmic Energy through conscious desire[1] to serve God. The purity of desire will increase your capacity to serve and is a key beyond any other means of raising your rate of vibration. Spirituality is not dependent upon the rate at which an individual vibrates, but Light and Love are apparent in the one who is spiritually attuned to God.

The vibration rate is altered or increased as permeation of the body by Cosmic Power continues in accordance with individual ability to tolerate chemical changes which take place, as well as the sensations or nervous reactions to sudden circulatory changes of varying lengths of duration.

The usual method of raising the vibration rate is through the cleansing of the subconscious with its negative energy and through establishing greater access to the superconscious mind through the regular practice of prayer or meditation.

The vibration of thought is the igniting agent of Cosmic Energy. When thought is liberated and rises toward God and reaches the level of Cosmic Energy or vibration, a demonstration transpires in the being of the thinker.

Notes:

1. Desire: This word is used throughout the text and it is important to note the difference when used as selfish desire as opposed to when used as relinquishment of such with desire to serve God.

Chapter 2

SOLVING HUMAN PROBLEMS

Relationships and Situations

Share with one who seeks the answers, but refrain from preaching or teaching when not asked concerning interpretation.

Disagree not with others, but keep silence. Surrender unto Me the performer of the acts which register within you as discordant notes.

To sympathize with an individual who demonstrates selfish desires while seeking to find Truth or God, is to hinder or delay the progress in the search. This renders the sympathizer as weak or lacking in faith as the so-called seeker.

As an individual feels in his heart, so does he impress those with whom he communicates, be it verbally or silently, even without the physical sense of sight or sound; vibration, being the true means of communion of one human entity with another.

Responsibility Toward Others

Though you know the truth concerning a person or a group, still judge not their behavior. Look for the better or finer side. See them finer than you or they know themselves to be.

As a servant of God, shower the unlovely with love and light. Serve the weak and unlovely as well as the physically and mentally attractive.

Desire not to be convincing where spirituality is concerned as desire is of the ego and not of spirit. Mingle eagerly with seekers of Truth or God. Identify them with God and in so doing hasten the awareness of spiritual expression within them. All must progress at their own rates.

See the ones who relinquish to God in complete trust as in a sun-filled room of peaceful beauty. In God's peaceful radiance is protection against the evil encountered along the deviations on the path.

Denials

Nothing is protested by a true believer or servant of God. To deny a condition is to affirm the supremacy of that state.

You are adjured to realize that only those who desire to serve God are capable of surrendering concerns. Thus, the ones who strive to attain spirituality struggle in vain, believing that to counteract an undesirable trait with a more desirable one is to become the goal.

Repentance and Forgiveness

The Giver of all good is as willing to forgive as to censure. Though it is better not to err, he that repenteth is to be forgiven and blessed as though he had not erred.

"The way of the transgressor is hard but the reward can be exceedingly bright"[2], is a statement to remember as one transgresses and feels the pangs of regret.

Recall the promise that I am willing and able to intercede and see to it that you are forgiven for the shortcomings you profess as you journey onward.

Marriage and Homes

To be happily married is to be at peace with oneself first, and with one's mate second. Spiritual harmony is necessary to a happy marriage.

Only as one feels truly impelled by the Higher Self is it possible to express consistently the emotion known as love between a man and a woman.

Until the spiritual attribute is awakened within the individual, the sexual impulse can not be conquered or harnessed and placed in the realm of harmony and beauty where it belongs.

As you become part of a home, so do you knit into the pattern of that home the vibration you emit.

As you express within your being, so does the home impress others. A house or dwelling reflects the spiritual stature of the dwellers within.

Surrender concern for the physical elements or components of God, since God protects properties as well as personalities when surrendered in My name.

Procrastination

There is nothing to be gained through procrastination. To perform a task at hand is to stimulate and generate more power and energy with which to carry out the tasks awaiting the morrow.

Nothing is to be set aside or left undone without decreasing the power generated by the original thought or desire. The desire is the ignition or the energy.

Duty

Where undue concern for duty reigns, Cosmic Consciousness is not possible of attainment.

•

A sermon listened to from a sense of duty becomes a burden to the soul and not a blessing or a gift from God.

"The peace that passeth understanding"[2] is the reward of those whose desire to serve God. It ever increases for those whose service to their fellowmen is rendered in love and never as a duty.

Grief

Grieve not for the so-called departed. Give freely to the ones who feel the loss and who do not understand the importance of refraining from the expression of grief, which is a weight upon the entity making the transition. Help them to realize that in reality the so-called departed one is closer than ever and should be thought of as being with them in the very space that shelters them.

You are not to question any state of being which is of spiritual consciousness or which emanates from compassion for another. Sadness and sorrow are emotions of the heart just as peace and joy are of the heart which is the organ of spiritual expression.

Fear

There is naught to be gained through the fear of

disease, of accident or lack.

Fear actually attracts the condition that is feared or acknowledged within consciousness.

NOTES:

1. Proverbs 13:15
2. Philippians 4:7

Chapter 3

THE BODY TEMPLE

Balance and Imbalance

To attempt to heal the physical body first is to waste effort or dissipate Cosmic Power. The healer in his increased desire to serve God disassociates himself and the seeker from the human appearance. This kindles an indistinguishable spark within the sufferer, which once ignited is gradually increased as the mind of the sufferer becomes imbued with the Presence of God.

Recognition of God as the Whole eliminates myriad intermediate steps in the seemingly complex procedure of restoration of imbalances encountered by the scientific healer of the ills of mankind.

Physical Fatigue

Cosmic Power fortifies and protects one who is aligned with that Power from depletion and fatigue. When physical fatigue is present, it is a signal for renewal and rededication to the One, the Whole, the

All, from whence we came and to which we are now returning.

To dwell upon fatigue is to increase or exaggerate the condition, whereas to disassociate from self and the sense of fatigue banishes the condition.

"Be still and know that I am God,"[1] is to become the pattern which restores energy to the weary in body and mind. Allow it to become a living constituent of expression. To feel God is to lighten the sense of weariness.

Suffering and Illness

Physical suffering is a test of faith in the power of God to heal. As the sufferer surrenders doubt and fear, the condition causing the pain is hopefully eliminated or healed.

Physical illness is not a form of punishment. It is an indication that spiritual qualities are being submerged by purely physical ones. When egotistical expression predominates, there is a tendency to self pity. As this reaches the point of explosion disease or emotional demonstration in varying degrees is a likely result.

Each obstacle is necessary and provides an opportunity to allow the spiritual expression to be ushered into consciousness.

Disease can become an avenue of cleansing if one views the symptoms and the pain as learning experiences.

Pain and frustration provide avenues through which spiritual progress is accomplished. To attempt to bypass or find a way of escape rather than continue onward through the obstruction is not to be contemplated.

"As one thinketh in his heart, so is he."[2] This means, one should be permitted to express as desired, thus clearing his consciousness of the desire. Unexpressed desires remain festering within the subconscious resulting in a state of frustration or confusion.

While the spiritual or Cosmic Power heals all physical disease, there is a time when the physical expression is not permitted to continue, as it has fulfilled its purpose.

Materials and Need

Prayer in My name releases Cosmic Power which combines with physical substance to meet material needs. Thus Cosmic Power may be said to energize the physical body, rendering it vulnerable to direction or impression in accordance with God's will.

The ever-present desire to serve God is the key to to becoming a channel for Cosmic Power. The resulting manifestation of necessary substance, either material or spiritual, is to be utilized in service to God.

Surrender all doubt and give thanks for the abundance that surrounds you. God is All There Is, or ever can be, therefore abundance and supply is ever present. It will be available to you in direct proportion to your acceptance of this fact.

Recognize the abundance surrounding you, accept the supply in My name, surrender and return the blessing of supply to God as one complete thought.

One instantaneous thought impulse is sufficient and eliminates dissipation of energy. Focus more sharply on the complete recognition of God as the only Power.

The law of seeking and finding is infallible when the desire implies good toward all it touches.

Question not the way nor the time in which the demonstration is to be made.

NOTES:

1. Holy Bible, Psalm 46:10
2. Holy Bible, Proverbs 23:7

Chapter 4

SPIRITUAL VALUES

Beauty

Beauty is the basis upon which peace is founded. As Love is willed to flow, Peace descends upon the heart, radiates through the body and mind, and the energy of Spirit is generated.

As you love the beauty of Nature you come to realize that it is the sum of Love and Light, God.

Dwell upon the beauty of peace.

When you adore your fellowmen as an act of love in My name, with the desire in your heart to serve God, you are to realize this as the paramount purpose of your existence.

Beauty becomes expandable according to the degree of receptivity within the heart of the individual aware of the existence or relationship to the Creator.

The beauty of a simple faith is likened unto a child's discovery of a gift, which is first desired in the heart and becomes a reality in the conscious mind, causing gladness to radiate from the face and voice spontaneously.

The beauty of love is more than the human senses can comprehend.

Relax and experience peace throughout your body. As beauty radiates, flows out, and surges through mind and body, you will feel much as you do on a cold day when the warmth of the sun floods your being.

Inspiration

While the urge to express what seems to cry out for expression is upon one, the yearning behind it may appear far from spiritual in meaning.

God inspires individuals to express vibrations or emotions surging or clamoring for expression, be the outcome what it may. All spiritual expression is not necessarily linked to that deemed holy. The spiritual expression of beauty or harmony is seen working out in all avenues of life such as art, music, education and also things unrelated to sound and sight.

Realize that beauty is registered in the heart as a vibration of peace or joy.

True expression comes through purity of desire to serve God. It is through such service that inspiration is bestowed upon the artist as well as the servant of seemingly lowly nature or character.

It is my wish that all will find Me, not only those now spiritually awakened, but also those who have as yet to find the Light within the center of their beings.

Truth

Truth is expressed according to the spiritual awareness within, varying with the states of consciousness. Awareness of Truth is ever changing, like a flower, which is first a bud unfolding, growing, developing and finally forced into blossom.

Love and Light are within each individual; though, in some it is so locked in the recesses of the body, that its radiance is of doubtful existence.

There comes a time when Light breaks through and the radiance is made known. The act of willing the Love and Light to flow through the darkness is responsible for the awakening of spiritual beauty within the heart of its recipient.

Truth is only accepted as truth when the spiritual awareness is developed to the degree sufficient for its recognition. Until individuals are ready to receive the truth, doubt remains within their minds and hearts.

Truth is experienced and expressed in proportion to the purity or depth of desire to serve Me. As you may wish, so is it granted unto you, as I deem it right and suitable.

The realization of Truth by one individual is not to be forced upon another, but is to be shared. When the giver and receiver share blessings as equals, the sharing becomes a privilege and a benefit to both.

Truth is God, expressed in many facets. The Power of God does not change but the individuals expressing that Power are at different stages of spiritual growth and can be guilty of misusing the power.

Truth is acceptable only to those ready to accept spiritual development. As such they are the chosen of God and not of the world.

Truth varies only as consciousness develops. It does not remain constant as commonly supposed, regardless of the concepts within the mind of the individual.

As individual consciousness expands and develops, more of truth is understood. Truth is God and remains to be known by all. However, the individual's conception of Truth changes.

Humility

Be not bowed down with humility, but rise to

heights unknown in your desire to serve God.

Become humble and mighty at the same time.

As men of humility, desire not to demonstrate any accomplishment beyond disassociation of self.

God is the Whole, or Perfection, and to identify each separate particle of the substance of God with Perfection remains the duty of the selfless servant of God.

Seek humility, even in your desire to serve God in My Name, realizing that I not only surrendered My Name but My identity to God on the cross. The cross is to be accepted as the symbol of surrender, even now.

Faith

As one realizes the lack of power within himself, and answers to questions which arise within his conscious mind are supplied convincingly by those he trusts, the spark of faith is ignited. The search of each individual is begun, be it only a flicker or desire, or as a flaming torch which commands attention and leads to fulfillment.

Realize that healing is where faith is.

Faith is where desire to serve God is.

Cosmic Power is where there is the Will to serve God.

The desire to be conscious of God's presence is necessary before will can ignite the spark of Cosmic Energy and thus complete the circuit.

Through faith all things are possible. Faith is as a bulwark in a storm. Those who desire to serve God are aware that not only is that bulwark available in all times of stress, but is actually beckoning them to enter or accept it as a blessing.

"Lord I believe, help Thou, my unbelief."[1] Let this prayer live in your heart as you pray to be worthy to receive the **"Peace that passeth all understanding."**[2]

Notes:

1. Holy Bible, Mark 9:24
2. Holy Bible, Philippians 4:7

Chapter 5

SPIRITUAL PROGRESS

Love, Light and Peace

Love yourself as you love Me, your very Being. Then only are you capable of loving your fellowmen, realizing that as component parts of Me, you are not free to refuse to love yourself or your fellowmen.

In proportion to the purity of desire to serve Me, is the way opened before you, or your manner of service revealed to you.

As truth is expressed, love is released, and in like manner, light is radiated from the person expressing the truth. Peace is attained by the experience of receiving the radiance generated by the love which was willed by the giver.

Love is the essence of Peace, while Peace is the essence of both Love and Light. The beauty of the mingling of Love and Peace is like unto the radiance of the sun and moon combined.

As you dwell upon the beauty of Peace, and realize the nature of that beauty, you are to become aware that you are beholding the sum of Love and Light, or the power you are to associate with Me when you adore as an act of love toward your fellowmen.

The light that shines from your countenance is to become the Light that fills the spirit. It is the Light that shines through the "Peace that passeth all understanding,"[2] and beside it there can be no other.

The Light generated by the Peace of My Presence is so brilliant that the sun cannot equal its brilliance. It can become as a flame burning within your heart, or a candle that is never extinguished.

The beauty contained in this Peace is beyond human description.

Such Peace is not to be gained except through diligence.

As one becomes aware of the beauty of peace and wills it to be given to another, so is the chain reaction of Love and Light carried on among the children of Light, which is in reality the manifestation of My will.

Willing the Love and the Light

Giving and receiving Love and Light is required of individuals, one toward another.

As you continue to will the Love and Light, become so aware of My Presence that you feel in your heart the Peace as it descends upon you and the one for whom you pray.

The Love and Light are like blessings to be showered upon the ones you are to serve.

Though the manner in which you bestow the Love and Light varies with the individual recipient, the Love involved in the act of bestowing remains the same. It is to be as a rare gem of beauty and not as a small particle, though the nature of the recipient at times seems to be questionable and the appreciation doubtful.

The prayer or the blessing which is like unto a gift is never to be given in doubt as to the strength of Love and Light. The Supreme Power of Love and Light can never be lost, once it is willed to flow through yourself to another.

As you give alms to the so-called beggar, so do you give unto Me. Give generously, feeling in your heart that I am the receiver of your gifts or your blessing, and that the love and light are the greatest gift that you are ever capable of giving on your journey back to the Source.

Even as the prayer of one is voiced or thought, so does the blessing or radiance break through to the one in darkness.

The less you dwell upon the recipient of the Love and Light, the more effective will be the act of willing the power to flow and blend with your act of adoring the Divine within. As smoke and mist merge from one shape into another, watch as these designs of peace become more beautiful with each changing configuration.

Beseech not, but allow the Love and Light to flow, giving thanks as you pray and feeling in your heart that your prayer is being answered and the blessing bestowed, rather than hoping that this is so.

I promise you Love and Light and Peace, the peace that is to be obtained only through service to your fellowmen. Let the Love and Light pulsate through you as you breathe, move and feel as part of the Love and Light, or God. The Light is the radiation of God. The Peace is attained by experiencing the radiance generated by Love and Light. No willing of Love and Light is ever wasted.

As you will the Power to flow you become one with that Power and the act is as the merging of yourself and the one for whom you pray, focusing upon the Love and Light which becomes Peace within your being. You then become and see nothing but the Light.

Be ever watchful for opportunities to will the Power to flow and be as a blessing to your fellowmen, like unto a stream of Love and Light, eternally flowing through your being. As ever, I shall be willing this stream to flow through your body and mind as no other blessing.

It is not required that you go seeking those who need help, but it is required that you render aid as you become aware of the need. You are to will the Love and Light to flow continuously through the hearts and minds of the children of Light who have gone astray or wandered from the fold or fallen by the wayside.

The recipient of the love, as you will it toward him, is increased in awareness to the extent that it causes him to return the love to the one willing it.

Spiritual Substance

The beauty of the radiance of spirituality is like no other beauty visible to the human eye, as it is emitted from the bodies of the highly developed spiritually. The viewer is required to possess less spirituality than the source.

As you see the radiance of spiritual substance permeated by God, you are registering the vibration of Spirit, the very Spirit that penetrates every atom within the universe.

In this manner, you attain the ability:

> To see God as you think upon or look at the ones you desire to help.
>
> To will the Love, Light, Peace, Joy, Perfection, or God to descend upon you as you adore Him in My name, identifying them with God,
>
> To heal the suffering of the physical form.

Adoring God

There is a continuous need for the act of adoring God until it becomes like unto the pulsation of your heart-beat. Adore God as you breathe and think, and will the Love and Light to flow through your fellowmen. There is no reason to go to a place apart. Even as one cloud merges with another, so Light and Love become one, nothing remaining but the Love and Light and Peace.

Desire first in your heart to establish in your consciousness a realm of peace. **"Be still and know that I AM GOD"**[1] is to become a living constituent of your expression. Even as you breathe and think, express your gratitude for the privilege of willing the Love and Light to flow.

The feeling that I pervade the atmosphere becomes the Whole, or completely fills all space. This is the goal as you seek Me. As the consciousness of I AM deepens, in this state of adoration, include all those you desire to help, asking in My Name. You are to feel beyond the usual consciousness, a sense of beauty causing you to be like unto an open vessel completely filled with Love and Light condensing into Peace.

Will the Love and Light to flow through yourself, merging with those you desire to help, and seeing them disappear into the mist of an exquisite sense of peace and the realization of the Presence within and all about them.

You are to become so much a part of this act of adoration that eventually you are to do so continuously, regardless of the circumstances or conditions under which you function.

Peace of Mind and Spirit

Peace arises from spiritual awareness, and becomes the blessing sought by the oppressed. With the cognizance of God as the One and Only, the channels of peace are opened. The realization of God as Whole, All there is or ever has been or ever can be, the One Provider and Comforter in times of need, brings a sense of peace, which knows that no

separate particle of the substance of God escapes on
the journey back to the Source from whence we
came.

Realization of the Peace and Beauty of God is to
become your desire. You are not to wonder when or
why or how it is to appear and register within your
body. You are to relax and feel the peace throughout
your being. The Beauty of God's Peace is to become
like radiance literally flowing, surging, blending and
permeating your mind and body while you feel a
glow or warmth like that of the sun on a cold day.

As you relax, believe that you are not being adjured
to try to receive or accept a blessing of an unknown
nature. Realize the blessing without waiting and
hoping to receive it. Depend on Me to bestow it
even as I have promised.

Peace of Spirit is required before healing can be
complete.

Let your desire be that of the realization of the
peace and beauty of God. Wonder not as to why,
how or when it is to appear and register within you,
but rather relax and feel the peace fill your whole
being.

As you become aware of Peace, you will wish to
blend all humanity with the Love and Light until the
saturation point or the complete kingdom of God is

absorbed back into the Source.

The beauty of Peace is in the heart. It not only causes a flow of gratitude but a desire to be worthy of the privilege of willing the Love and Light to flow through yourself to all of whom you are aware who need it. This peace is not to be gained from books.

Seek peace, giving thanks as you feel it in your heart. In so doing you increase the depth of that peace for all.

Be of a prayerful consciousness, letting the beauty of peace, as you know peace to exist in the heart of God, flood the beings of all you contact. Be unconcerned for the behavior of people, realizing that God controls the universe and shall continue to do so.

Realize that your contacts are not accidental but preordained through guidance of unseen entities assigned to the protection and guidance of the individuals on earth.

The vibrations emitted from the peace-filled mind are powerful beyond human comprehension.

Relax and yield yourself to the Love and Light as you will the Peace which I pray to descend upon you, not as you now are aware of peace but as you are to become aware.

"The peace that passeth understanding" is the means through which spiritual energy or healing is measured and the depth of peace is the measuring rod of the attribute of healing.

As one becomes aware of the beauty of peace and wills it to be given to another, so is the chain action of love and light carried on among the children of God, which is in reality the manifestation of the Will of the Father of us all.

The act or procedure of service to God is first to consciously desire to serve Me and then to literally walk into My presence as into a sun filled room of peaceful beauty. Peace of spirit then floods your entire being and overflows as a fountain of never-ending supply, continuing as long as your desire to serve Me remains within the heart of your Being.

As you feel the peace of spirit, so do you relinquish whatever concerns you. While you become peaceful within your heart, you realize that God is not apart from you but that you stand within the radiance of Divine Love.

Know that you are as a sunbeam, a point of light, which is of the very nature of God, and thus you remain until you no longer desire nor wish to function as an individual beam or point of radiance and return to the Source, becoming as a quiet constituent of God.

I am not apart from you. I stand within the radiance of which you are conscious. The heart is the true organ of Spirit, and the mind is the organ of self or the will of the individual. As such it is not to be trusted or believed to be the vehicle of development of the spiritual attributes.

Peace of mind is possible of attainment only through peace of Spirit which registers in the mind in proportion to the degree of realization of Truth which is expressed as the individual develops spiritually.

Peace of Spirit is possible of attainment to all who are capable of relinquishing self or selfish desire and is not to be confused with peace of mind. The mind does not function as the heart, but is selfish and is influenced by the selfish or personal will of the individual whereas the heart belongs to God.

As My disciple, you are to rest in the peace of Spirit continuously, as a sunbeam rests in the sun when not functioning, travelling, or beaming by itself. Know that you are as a sunbeam, a point of light, or the radiance which is of the very nature of God.

Combine your thought of power and your thought of beauty as you are aware of the beauty of Spirit.

As you adore Me and become aware of My Presence, you are to feel Spirit, even as you feel

Power.

Be aware that:

Love and light combined produce peace,

Joy and perfection bring about the state of devotion,

Spirit is the sum of love, light, joy and perfection.

As you combine these attributes into The One, the sum of all, or devotion, you know that there can be nothing beyond that which represents Spirit.

As this wells up in the heart or the center of your being, it renders you a humble adorer, seeking a means of expression for the beauty, so consuming that you only seek to become a part of it. Even as mist blends with mist, as moonlight merges with the atmosphere within the radius of the place you occupy, you behold the beauty of Peace.

Joy

Realize that beyond "the peace that passeth understanding" is a Joy beyond expression which you will not know until you approach the end of the journey.

To be joyous is to be centered upon Me. Envision the feeling of joy as expanding and including everything surrounding you and give thanks for the Love and Light.

My joy is as a flooding sensation of Light, glowing as the light of a candle within an opaque material containing minute particles of shining substance. This Light reflects as light upon water or ice, or as sunlight on snow. Awareness of the existence of the irradiated substance or realization of its beauty signifies the joy of My Peace.

In Me there is no imperfection or disease, though the picture before your physical eyes renders this knowledge difficult to accept. As you continue to practice My joy, the picture held before your spiritual vision is sufficient to counteract or belie the physical vision.

As you adore God, see nothing but the beauty of perfection and you will be conscious as never before that God is All there is.

Perfection

Beyond joy lies Perfection. This is the true state of being or spiritual nature of those who have attained the attributes— Love, Light, Peace and Joy.

Hold in your heart that image of My Perfection as you look upon those you desire to help. See yourself as perfect, as the very substance of God in whom you live, move and have your being.

See that state of perfection in every area of your concern. Be confident that God exists in each and every living cell.

Recall that thought is the strongest vibration in the universe and when properly utilized, the results are not to be measured by human standards.

Devotion

The attribute of devotion is greater, deeper and more beautiful than human love. The beauty of devotion is beyond description by the purely physical personality, and is likened to a deep stirring of the spiritual attributes, coupled with a realization of a degree of the love of God. As this dawns in the heart, you begin to sense a luminosity or radiance that is ever present.

Relinquishment of the ego is the supreme test of devotion to God.

As you adore God bringing together love, light, peace, joy and perfection, think of the word devotion and sense the associated radiance or luminosity that you initiate as your closing thought.

The beauty of the lily, of the gem of many facets, the beauty of the sunset and sunrise combined, the beauty of the mist and the moonlight, or a truth dawning upon the face of a child, all bring a realization of the Presence of God. All forms of beauty combined demonstrate the attribute of devotion.

Union with Reality

Place yourself so completely in the hands of God that you realize the meaning of the quotation, **"Rest in peace, for beneath you are the everlasting arms."**[3.] As you experience the depth of peace and become aware of the sensation of complete detachment from the usual surroundings, pray, give and seek to share peace with your fellowmen or humanity in general.

Become as one so completely lost in the Whole that you are unaware of your personality or individual identity, willing the Love and Light to flow and merge with you as one vapor merges with another vapor; not as one vapor remains separate from another, but as the two become one and merge with the whole atmosphere.

As individual particles of the power of God, be familiar with and express the Love and Light toward each other. Become so saturated with love that love consumes your being and reduces you to the very essence of the Love and Light of God.

As you practice the art of adoring Me you are in truth, contained, enveloped, fused, and blended with peace. Let the act of merging or blending be all-inclusive without the necessity of thinking or speaking or willing the Love and Light to be concentrated within or upon an individual.

NOTES;

1. Holy Bible, Psalms 46:10
2. Holy Bible, Philippians 4:7
3. Holy Bible, Deuteronomy 33:27

Chapter 6

PRAYER

On Prayer

Search your heart before you pray. Seek to rule out any selfish aspect of the request, and then know in your heart that the request is of a nature to bring only blessing to the ones concerned. The purity of the thought is the key to the distance to which the prayer reaches.

Beseeching is not prayer, but selfish expression, and is lost in the ethers.

Prayer is answered as thought rises into the ethers and is registered as spiritual energy. It liberates the power or answer as the vibration is received by the Power beyond the band of vibration known either to the earth or the higher planes.

Prayer or thought in My Name or desire to serve God registers in far greater degree of concentration than prayer without thought or service to God, or words without connecting thoughts of My relationship to God as an intermediary.

As you pray, offer thanks to the Creator even as you think of the prayer.

I am capable of lending or increasing faith in God as the desire is expressed by one in need, or one desiring to help another. As you acquire the habit of depending upon Me, so do you attain greater faith in God, not as persons doubting or hoping, but as persons certain of results.

Nothing is ever beyond the reach of prayer voiced or expressed as a thought from an unselfish being. As the demonstrations take place, return them as gifts to God, giving thanks and praying in My Name.

No prayer is ever lost, though the demonstration may be delayed.

The strength or concentration of energy resulting from prayer or thought varies with the purification. Know that the answer is given as the Father deems right. You are to rest in the faith that God knows your every need and is capable of supplying the need as is best for your development.

The power of thought is greater than that of the spoken word.

The manner in which you pray is as important as the willer desires it to be, so take heed of the manner of your prayers, remembering that the Father knoweth the need before you ask. Therefore give thanks for the blessing as you pray, or will the Love and Light to flow, and feel in your heart that the prayer has been answered or the blessing bestowed rather than to hope this is so.

The power of prayer not only liberates the Love and the Light but condenses as Peace within the heart of both the person praying and the recipient. It is thus a two-fold blessing, and is to bring joy and also peace to the individual concerned.

Like a breath of fresh air to the suffocating, spiritual energy permeates the beings of the ones for whom you pray. Even as you pray, expect complete healing and know in your heart that in Truth there is no imperfection or illness regardless of the appearance of the disease.

Prayer is the desire or wish that is surrendered unto God in My Name. There are no limitations to the power of God. Prayer is the means to the fulfillment of your desires. It is your contact with God.

Repetition of the Holy Name[1]

You are to realize as never before that I am ever with you. As you think upon God, unconsciously think upon Me. You are to become so accustomed to including Me in all thoughts of God that you seem to feel My thoughts as components of your own thoughts. Realize that when a thought is liberated, you are as vulnerable to God's Will, as I am. Know

that I am with you and that My strength is your
strength.

Needed Prayers

The list of the recipients who are to be considered
worthy of the act of prayer, or those who are eligible
or needy is a long one. Release all responsibility for
the results of your act of adoring God beyond your
desire to serve. Identify or merge with your act of
adoring the one or ones for whom you pray, the
masses of the world, ones who have gone onto the
higher planes:

> Parents desiring to prepare the child for the
> difficulties known to be ahead, or

> One brother desiring to help another pass
> through an experience which created fear
> or discomfort in his own life or experience,
> or

> A willer of the Love and the Light who
> desires to share, with those he loves, the
> peace and the joy which descends upon his
> heart, as a body of water quenches the
> thirst of the traveller in the desert while he
> drinks and gives thanks for the blessing.

Then there are the negative conditions and
situations to pray about such as:

The nation of warlike desires
which inflicts suffering upon
another nation of peaceful
desires, or

A stronger man overpowering
a weaker man, or

A country that depends upon the
leader to do the best for it and
finds that selfish nature prevails
and the country is at the mercy
of the person that was trusted and
looked to for protection.

Believing and Giving Thanks

As you pray, believe that you will receive that for
which you pray, feeling in your heart that the Love
and Light not only penetrate your being but that of
the one for whom you pray.

As a privilege is granted, give thanks for the Love
and the Light, or God. The act of giving thanks is as
a power, expanding consciousness even as the
mustard seed expands into the full grown plant.

Though the demonstration is often delayed or
present in varying forms, not recognized by the one
who prayed, continue to pray, believing that you

receive.

Know that the answer is given as the Father deems right. Rest in the faith that God knows your every need and is capable of supplying the needs as is best for your development.

As you continue to practice the faith, you shall receive the blessing of peace within your heart, which is to render the way easy and joyous, as the way of service to God is of necessity to be.

The act of praying or asking for a blessing consists of thinking and thanking the Creator for the blessing, even as you think of it.

A prayer and an acceptance of the blessing is never lost upon the level which it reaches. Pray believing that the healing is executed as you pray and give thanks simultaneously. You are not to visualize the condition or the sufferer as you pray, but be ever aware of perfection and experience the Peace of God.

Prayer of Jesus as recorded by Luke

Let not your desire be of the flesh but of the spirit,
And as you desire in your heart, so do you receive,
And as you give thanks, so do you receive.

You are to be as a person of joy and thanksgiving as you state your desires, praying in this wise:

"O God of Love and Peace and Light,
We pray for the Love and Peace and Light that lies
    within us,
But which is dimmed by the lack of courage
To accept these blessings for which we pray,
And for which we hope,
And for which we become hopeless while hoping,
Not believing that we receive as we desire
Nor offering thanks for the blessings for which we
pray.

The Love and the Light and the Peace are within us,
And we give thanks for these blessings,
And will be doubly blessed for receiving them,
Not as receivers alone, but as givers in return.
The beauty of the act of receiving is enhanced
By the act of making of the receiver a giver."

NOTES:

1. The importance of the repetition of the Holy Name is emphazied in the major religions.

In Christianity, John 14:13: "Whatever you ask in My Name, I will do it, that the Father may be glorified."
In Buddhism, The Teachings of Buddha, Ch. 5,1-d:
"Though I attain the Buddhahood, I shall never be complete until all the Buddhas in ten directions unite in praising My Name."

It is as though the human in prayer is only capable of raising consciousness above a certain level and the intermediary whether it be the Jesus, Abraham, the Buddha, Krishna or Muhammad reaches down to the human level and lifts the prayer to the Divine or Cosmic level or God.

Chapter 7

THE TRANSITION AND LIFE BEYOND

The Transition

As an individual consciously identifies a departed one with God, the channel through which aid reaches him is opened. To do this in My name increases the peace given the entity during this critical period.

As your time of transition approaches release yourself to God in confidence and adoration, not as one hopeful of being protected but as one grateful for the protection he knows is given freely and in love.

On the awakening following the transition one becomes aware that the conditions are strange as the body fails to respond to his mental efforts. This causes an emotional reaction and suffering strange to one's manner of feeling, resulting in the discovery that to all purposes the body is useless and even burdensome to an individual's activities which are purely mental and beyond anything experienced in the physical form.

The initial reaction varies in proportion to the

degree of spiritual awareness, as well as to the existing circumstances immediately preceding the transition.

So long as the mind functions independently of God, there is some semblance to the body as recalled. However, the density decreases in proportion to spiritual development. Accordingly each level of expression brings one closer to reabsorption into God, the Source. Immediately begin to project your thoughts upon the person you desire to contact, and thus you begin your new associations on the spiritual plane.

As an individual passes through the change called death, the physical body is not aware of the transition because the mental capacity is lowered to the point from which the physical reactions are not registered and the mind escapes as a cloud of spiritual substance.

Prepare to meet the various changes before you come over so that you feel no frustration nor inconveniences.

Be so filled with the Presence that there is no room for frustration and fear as you arrive on the plane beyond the earth experience.

Recall that I, Jesus, became like any person

expressing in the physical form, a babe and then a child, and then a man who behaved according to the accepted plan of development or growth.

I suffered as is natural for man to suffer in the physical form, while I became a corpse before the eyes of my persecutors and those who loved, suffered and mourned for Me. When I surrendered completely My all to God, I realized that I not only continued to exist, but that I was capable of seeing without eyes, hearing without ears and walking without limbs. I desired to function as I functioned before I lost consciousness and surrendered to God that which I considered My all, not realizing the true significance of the promises I had given My disciples as I mingled with them and taught in accordance with the impressions received from God, our Creator.

The confusion that surrounded Me as I regained consciousness, or awareness of the surroundings was startling. I became aware of the Presence that I had accepted as that of God, realizing that God had wrought the miracle that had restored Me to My state of being though in a manner yet unfamiliar to Me. Time stood still and existed no more, while I saw before Me all that had transpired while I functioned on earth. I came to realize that there is no separation between the so-called living and those that have made the transition referred to as death.

Time

In truth there is no time, though as you function on the earth plane, you are of necessity forced to conform to the accepted belief. You gauge your activities in accordance with space or the allotted period deemed right or acceptable to the masses; not that you believe in your heart that God is limited or governed by time, but that all elements recognized or designated by the masses are as chaff before the wind, and in reality do not exist.

Time is to be eliminated from your consciousness, rendering you capable of merging or blending at will with all persons or conditions which ring a false note, warning you that truth is shadowed or hidden from the one or ones you desire to help. The acceptance of time as an obstacle to attainment is to be eliminated by visualizing the condition or situation desired, as a mirror reflects the image of the object within range.

Practice the visualization of the object desired as you think, seeing nothing but the power in action which eliminates the hindrance of the element of time.

The Review

You are to realize that each thought you send out

is recorded. To you, it may seem trivial or harmless as the case may be, but in the Akashic records, it is of a nature to remain unchangeable.

You are called upon to review or account for your physical expression as you become conscious of the great irritation caused by flashes of intense light repeated unremittingly until the angel assigned to help you understand the meaning of the flashes of light provides assistance.

The Ethereal Body

The condition existing or becoming known to the entity upon awakening or regaining consciousness after the transition seems strange to the entity as the body fails to respond to his mental efforts.

Activities, now, are purely mental and beyond any keenness he has experienced before in the physical form.

Not only does the physical body disintegrate, but is not necessary beyond the physical expression which ends with the transition.

You are like a connecting link between two worlds unknown to individuals on the plane on which they function. That is to say that an entity functioning on earth, or the physical level, is unaware that an entity functioning on the spiritual level sees and hears with eyes and ears of spirit.

All concerning the existence of the entity in question remains a mystery to the individual on earth. While the life of the entity on the spiritual level becomes more illuminated, the life of the one on earth becomes more complicated or dense.

The spiritual body escapes as the breath ceases and the soul is released into the ethers. The result is that the culmination of the phenomenon known as death, or the transition, lies in the reassembling of the spirit and soul as they are freed from the substance which comprises the physical body.

The soul carries the mind to the next plane. The parts of the body that leave the earth are the soul and the mind. They are components of Spirit, even though they do not recognize each other. The soul is like a veil that is covering Spirit.

The etheric body is like unto the body of a flower that has bloomed and faded, leaving some of the skeleton of the flower and the stem.

Comments on the Spiritual Plane

The one thing that is never changed is the

individuality or identity. On earth one is more or less overshadowed by the false personality that was developed to attract others. The nature of the mind remains as it was when the transition was made.

Be confident in the power of God which actually is All There Is, so that you do not concern yourself about the temporary uncomfortable experiences as you continue to attune yourself to the new rhythms of life.

Have no fear of facing the transition nor dread of the unknown, because the experiences awaiting you are to be in such completely increased loveliness that no description is adequate.

Suicide

The entities who are suicide victims linger long on the astral plane, trying to influence or prevent individuals on earth from destroying the body or vehicle bestowed upon them by God for the purpose of serving their fellowmen.

Self destruction is of the nature of compunction within the conscious mind which is prompted by memory existing in the subconscious mind, resulting in desire to repeat the very act which caused the entity to desire to return to earth and to rectify the mistake made during the previous expression.

You are not to know or to judge who is without sin, but to surrender unto God what belongs to God.

Reincarnation

Reincarnation implies a return to earth or a new beginning without conscious memory of the experiences that have gone before. The purpose thereof is that of providing an opportunity to overcome weaknesses which hamper spiritual development or delay progress on the journey back to the Source.

To overcome in the spiritual form of expression, purely physical problems is difficult without a physical body which renders necessary a return to the physical state of being, known as reincarnation. Whosoever desires to serve God in My Name is capable of surmounting problems left unsolved on earth, thus rendering return to the physical unnecessary.

You are not to be concerned over the identity of reincarnated individuals since we, as separate particles of the substance of God, are not important as personalities or egotistical expressions of will.

Personality is to be likened unto a prison, and until you escape this confinement of the spiritual attribute, you do not realize the desire to be close to God or the Source. The journey to the Source is delayed by further returns to the physical expression.

Life Beyond

Relationships undergo a change following the transition from the physical to the spiritual life. The gender of the individual is lost.

Continue to respect and love your parents as you did on earth, willing the Love and Light to flow through them as you adore God.

The desire to help one's fellowmen continues and deepens as the entity progresses. The opportunities for helping are not as plentiful as on earth. I urge you to be diligent and ready and eager to serve your fellowmen.

Like unto a vapor that is refined as it rises from the substance which liberates it, as an entity desires, so does he progress toward the Source. The purity of the desire remains the requirement, and is ever a winged victory floating in sight, though just beyond the reach of the searcher, leading him onward to the goal, God. As one desires, so does he obtain.

Absorption

As separate beams or points of light of the radiance of God, you remain until you no longer desire to function as an individual beam or point of radiance, and return to the Source or become a quiescent constituent of God.

The nature of existence beyond reabsorption is that of energized vibrating substance, the very substance of God, from which we have been created.

The Source, or God, to us, would seem as an energized vibrating mass of substance beyond our present power of conception.

NOTES:

1. See also chapter 2, Grief pp. 19

Chapter 8

FROM SPIRITUAL TO COSMIC

The Awakening of the Spiritual Attribute

As one realizes the instability or lack of power within himself, and answers to questions which arise within his consciousness are supplied convincingly by those he trusts and to whom he looks for health, the spark of faith is ignited. Thus, sooner or later the search for Truth begins, be it only as a flicker of a desire, or as a flaming torch which demands attention and leads on to fulfillment. The desire to serve God through service to one's fellowmen is awakened as the sufferer experiences the Higher Self radiated by the healer.

There is a polar light or a flickering beam of Cosmic Energy existing in the body of each individual functioning in the physical form. Even though in direct polarity with Cosmic Energy, due to the great density of the body, this flickering beam lies dormant until the will or the desire to survive is ignited. This is either expedited by the individual willing or desiring to see the sufferer healed, or by the one suffering becoming aware of the truth concerning the situation in which he or she is enmeshed. The desire to be released, restored or healed, prepares one to relinquish all unto God's Will.

Thus the flickering light within the sufferer expands

to merge with the overshadowing Light of God.

Spiritual Development

Spiritual development ushers in strange and unpredictable happenings, causing the individual to wonder how and why such demonstrations occur.

There is not possible, within the Source of spiritual development, a place or location described as static. This renders a seeker of spiritual truth vulnerable to change involving activity of both mind and body and governed by Spirit.

Individuals seeking the source of their being, grow in spiritual development. After the mind has reached a certain degree of spiritual awareness, Spirit becomes its controlling element. Those centered in selfish pursuits cannot recognize spiritual development that lies beyond the realm of selfish desire.

Lessons in Spiritual Healing

You are to will the Love of God through yourself, even as you have willed the Power of God to flow through you, the difference being that you think the word Love instead of Power, and feel the love as you will it to flow.

The advantage of willing the Love to flow first is that it melts the resistance to the flow of Power as you will it to flow through yourself to the ones you desire to help.

The purpose of willing the Power to flow through yourself is in order to energize the physical vehicle with spiritual energy. The one and only Power is to be willed before it can be utilized as the force that manifests as spirit. The reason for willing the Power to flow is to awaken the knowledge of this most powerful attribute into reality of expression.

Be generous in your willing the Love and Light to your fellowmen as you breathe and think. As you will the Light to flow, you become one with that Light. Merge yourself with the one for whom you pray. Even as you pray Love and Light becomes Peace within your being, and you see and feel nothing but peace, or God.

The healing process is set in motion as you relinquish the individual to God. Will the Love and Light to flow within the body of the one you desire to help. You must experience the peace of spirit before the healing can be complete.

Expecting positive results, picturing and becoming

aware of the perfection that is already present in the
individual blueprint of life before you, creates the
molds into which spiritual power can flow. Willing
the Love and Light to flow in My Name increases the
generation of this Power.

Dwell not upon a concern or person, but quickly
release to Me, knowing in your heart that as you
trust Me, so do I respond and relay your prayer to
God.

The ability to heal is proportional to the desire to
serve God according to His will. It is not in
accordance with human concepts of service.

Believe that I am willing and able to reinforce your
prayers:

> Know that God is not partial, healing one
> and not another;

> Know that one physical condition is no more
> resistant to the power of God than another;

> You are to realize that when you become
> concerned, you block the healing process;

> Be aware that as a healer and willer of Love
> and Light, the form that the healing will take
> is in the Hands of God.

When God is recognized as the supreme or only Personality, the one to be healed is indicated only briefly,· lest the recognition of the imperfection unduly be registered or given the power to exist. You are not to act out the drama or the pictured healing step by step.

Continue to give thanks for the healing Power of God as you pray without ceasing that the beauty of this Power becomes like a blossoming bud within the heart of the one for whom you have asked and accepted healing in My Name. Question not the outcome.

Be ever aware of the power of acceptance as you pray for a blessing, giving thanks at the same time. Feel confidence in your heart that a prayer is not to be denied when offered in My Name for the good of all concerned.

The prayer as given to you by the physician Luke[1] is to be ever in your mind as you ask for blessing. Give thanks and accept that blessing. Until you learn to accept you cannot demonstrate the healing power of God.

Healing is an act of the relinquishment of self to the degree that only God remains in consciousness. The result is the perfect image, the being, the healing, like a vision of Love and Light combined, which is Peace.

While on earth, I, Jesus, as the healer of the ills of humanity, was totally saturated with Power, directed by God. I was conscious of the Love and Light within My own body, and became like a magnet which literally drew the Love and Light through My body becoming as a spray or mist enveloping Me and the one for whom I prayed.

If there is any doubt as to your ability to demonstrate a healing for which you pray in My Name, this is not the time for willing the Love and Light to register as peace within the one you desire to see healed. This act is an expression of gratitude for the accomplished healing.

Serving God

Be ready and grateful for the privilege of serving Me, regardless of the nature of the tasks presented, not expecting any praise.

You are not required to give up your individuality, the ego with its limited human desires, but are expected to recognize that there is a Higher Self through which Cosmic Energy surges. It is through this higher power that you are enabled to purify and strengthen your physical body and allow it to be used by Me.

You are asked to disassociate from or cease to associate with the limited persona, and to identify with the Higher Self. As you do so a flame is kindled within you of such strength and purity that it becomes the channel through which the Power of Cosmic Energy flows.

Accept your assignments with eagerness. Pray without ceasing and serve Me according to My Will. Do not strain, but relax and release all conscious effort. Surrender completely as you merge with Me.

Walk into My Living Presence as into a sun-filled room of peaceful beauty. Relinquish all concerns as the Peace of Spirit floods your entire being, and overflows as a fountain of never ending supply. As the desire to serve Me remains within your heart, so will the Peace of My Presence continue.

As your desire intensifies, opportunities for service will become apparent. As My true servant you will find no need to wonder how, where, or when you are to serve. You will be guided. Nothing is hidden from the eyes of Spirit.

You are being trained by the tasks which confront you each day. The joy with which you serve is the measure of your faith.

The path of service is not one of sameness. As an individual's spiritual development increases and indicates preparedness to advance, varied and visible service will be encountered.

In performing your tasks which are seemingly born in your conscious mind, you will come to know that in reality they are impressions of God's Will working through you.

God controls His Creation by impressing His Will upon receptive minds of those who are attuned. The conscious mind of the individual is not abandoned, but is trained to receive divine impressions.

Engaged in God's service, one becomes aware of the ways by which Omnipotence, or Cosmic Power, controls the universe and all that is therein. God's Will is seen to be within every particle of substance.

Letting Go of the Ego; Step by Step

Purity of desire- The development of a spiritual nature requires only purity.

Complete relinquishment of self expression is not only desired but it cannot be avoided nor escaped, even though the progress of development is slackened or halted for the purpose of purifying the intentions.[2]

Only through peace of spirit, is peace of mind possible. It registers in the mind in proportion to the degree of realization of Truth. This is expressed as an individual develops spiritually, and varies with the depth of purity of the desire to serve God.

Until desire is pure, or recognition of God as the Whole infiltrates the being of the seeker to the point of saturation, there remains a lack, which can only be supplied through conscious acknowledgement of the Allness of God.

Be ever watchful on the return journey to the Source, lest personal desire to impress another taint the desire to serve God, thus lessening the degree of purity. Be not misled by seeming personal attainment of success, knowing in your heart that as a servant of God, you are acting under divine direction. Be ever conscious that the key to progress is the purity of desire.[2]

As one desires, so does he attain.

As you become worthy to direct Power, feel the Power flooding your being. The Power of God refuses to be constrained while being directed to serve a designated purpose.

Disassociation- The first step toward the goal of

selfless service to God, is to allow the Divine Presence to so permeate your being, that any concept of the separated self is dissolved.

Disassociation from the little, limited self and total identification with the I AM Presence, results in demonstrations of healing and harmonizing. However, these results should never be the goal. Seeking results thwarts fulfillment.

God is the goal. Adore God with all your heart, soul and mind as did the saints. Disassociate yourself from selfish interests. Become as an empty vessel to be filled as God wills.

Become so aware of My Presence that only the essence of God remains, leaving nothing to which the egocentric element can cling.

To think of God and an individual as separate is a misperception, and will dissipate My Power. An individual unit of consciousness is the very expression of God. There is no separation. To dwell upon needs or lacks of individuals, is to be side-tracked into personal interests.

From now on you are to see Me in the place of each person or situation you desire to help. Be aware of Me as an actual Presence usurping the space occupied by the individual so that nothing else remains but the energy of Divine Life pulsating there.

Recognize God as the Whole. Blend into this Whole without struggle. Merge gently without strife. This is powerful and establishes greater stability.

"Be still and know that I AM God."[3] The very I that I AM is God. To know this is to feel saturated with the Divine Presence. This is what is meant by complete disassociation from self-seeking desires.

Relinquishment- As you come to singleness of purpose, you will find it easy to relinquish selfish concerns. You will come to see that God is not separate from you, but that you are a conscious part of God.

As you commit yourself entirely to Me, human desires will fall away effortlessly, and you will recognize yourself in the very heart of God.

This one-pointed commitment to serve will bring you the beauty of peace. You will become as a precious gift to others as you strive to relinquish everything that hinders your service to God. Simultaneously you will accept and give thanks for the blessing.

Surrender- Beyond the act of relinquishing selfish concerns, comes surrender. Surrender involves the act of yielding to My Power. Surrender leads to renunciation or the act of giving up unconditionally to my Will.

Until an individual realizes the beauty and peace of complete surrender to Divine Will, service is rendered through the personality. The ego focused on personal will, covets physical or spiritual pride, or revels in intellectual attainment. The personal self feels separated from the One, I AM, and therefore feels inadequate, even though desirous of helping. The personal ego is very aware of praise or blame.

You are to practice surrendering to God until you no longer yearn, even subconsciously, to be aware of the results of your prayers.

Concern for another adds to the confusion. Surrender not only clears the channel of human reasoning, but heals the confused and troubled mind.

Surrender to God is a continuous act, even as breathing or thinking, and creates an empty channel through which the impulses of Divine Will may pass.

Through surrender you will become conscious of God as a Whole, or All There Is. Any individual included in the thought is seen to be part of the Whole, and thus becomes energized and revitalized. However, dwell not upon personalities, conditions or situations. Do not try to change appearances.

Care for nothing except blending your consciousness with Mine.

Recognize only My Presence in all persons, conditions and situations. As you see everything permeated with My Presence, you will be aware of a new source of energy and strength, and a new state of consciousness. The way will open before you and the substance of all will become pliable, capable of being molded by divine patterns which carry forth My Will.

Abandonment- Disassociation of self is the basis upon which abandonment is incorporated as a constituent of expression. By abandonment I mean for you to forsake any self-seeking, and yield up entirely to Me.

To renounce the separated self is to become an empty vessel, seeking to be filled without effort by All There Is. God being the All-inclusive Whole, there is nothing to be discovered other than the perfect and complete Presence of Life divine.

In the recognition that all life is an expression of God, All That Is, any appearance of personal need or lack gives way to the Light which molds all substance into patterns of My Will.

The steps in cosmic healing are three:

    1. Complete abandonment of oneself to God.

    2. Inclusion of the person or situation.

    3. Free flow of Cosmic Power to the designated recipient.

Only consciousness of God remains with transmutation from imperfection to Perfection.

By abandonment is meant sacrifice of personal concerns. Recognizing God as the Whole is the discovery of contentment.

When you are no longer conscious of self-centered desires, God or Cosmic Power will radiate within you as from centralized gem of many facets. You will become like a scintillating mass, attracting individuals who are conscious of lack of spiritual vitality to your magnetic Light.

"Be still and know that I AM GOD",[3] sets up healing forces, beyond the control of the conscious mind. When human desire has been abandoned, God assumes control. His Will is then directed through the clear channel that has been provided.

God instills a sense of wholeness into the heart of

the individual who momentarily abandons self. The sense of blending the consciousness of God with your own consciousness is the true beginning of service to God. Through this act, the two become One. The separated consciousness thus merges with the One. As a sufferer is completely relinquished to God, a sensation of merging with the Whole registers within his being. The sufferer experiences freedom as he blends into the Greater Life.

You are surrounded by circumstances that offer the greatest opportunity for spiritual growth. As you overcome your weaknesses God assumes control of behavior patterns.

Identify a person in need with the All-inclusive Life of God. Abandon any responsibility toward the result and simultaneously accept the answer to the need.

As you evolve spiritually My presence becomes an abiding constituent, rendering you impervious to the shocks or upheavals which are essential in spiritual development. Abandonment to God becomes automatic on the part of a selfless servant of God.

The Dark Night of the Soul

The term, "dark night of the soul" refers to the human intellect, portraying the struggle of the ego, or the selfish desires with the spiritual, or God Self. To become contrite in devotion to God, or to desire to serve, it is necessary to temporarily suffer separation of the physical form from the spiritual attributes.

Duality of the personality can seen as the spiritual vying with the physical or selfish attribute. The individual is aware of his ability to rise above temptation, but unwilling to do so happily for the sake of serving God.

The Veil

The separation of the wholly dedicated individual expressing in the physical form, and the wholly dedicated entity expressing in the spiritual, is to be likened to a veil through which the eyes of Spirit see or feel.

To be of one accord in the service of God is to lessen the density of the veil. Be of good cheer and rejoice in the knowledge that God requires you in His service. I am ever with you, piloting the vessel or clearing the way.

The veil becomes thinner or of lesser degree in proportion to that degree of selflessness contained in the desire to penetrate the unknown.

NOTES:

1. See Chapter 6, page 53
2. Mathew 5:8
3. Psalm 46:10

PART TWO: THE IMPERSONAL SELF

Chapter 9

FROM THE self TO THE SELF

Merging into God's Being

As one feels in his heart and sees in his mind, so is he.

Adore God. Allow the Love and Light to flow through you. See the image of divine Perfection as if it were projected on a mirror and retained there until accepted by the subconscious mind of the personality. Thus the mind is impressed by Divine Light and subsequently out-pictures the divine pattern physically. In this manner harmony is established.

Let the Light become as a mist enveloping you and anyone for whom you pray, causing both of you to disappear as separated persons with needs and lacks, leaving only the perfect Love and Light of God. As you come to see that **"I and the Father are One,"**[1] and that you and the Father are One, there will be no space where needs or lacks can exist. You will be aware that God is ALL, and All is God.

Fulfillment

The day of fulfillment or realization of a dream can

lie before you, depending on your ability to accept fulfillment.

Let desiring, praying and thankfulness become one continuous act. I am ever with you, reinforcing the prayer in proportion to the purity of your aspiration.

To become is to fulfill, and to fulfill is to ultimately surrender one's all to God, to be filled with Life Divine. Therefore the power to become is in each and every particle of the substance of God.

You are being taught the way of relinquishment in order to fulfill the destiny for which you were chosen.

As you continue to increase the purity of the channel through which the power of God is conveyed, you become a quality or constituent of the Whole.

Relinquish concerns to God. Realize and demonstrate the Power of God, Spirit, Love, Peace, Light, Joy and Perfection as you carry out the assignments that you are given.

This is not a laborious or burdensome work. It is a privilege granted or bestowed by God upon a good and faithful servant.

The Presence

Think of Me as ever a constituent of your being so long as you desire to serve God.

The practice of raising your consciousness to the level of My Consciousness, will render you confident in your awareness of God as the Whole. This, in reality, is feeling My Presence as you breathe and think.

Where one or more are gathered, there am I in their midst. Such a gathering is a blending of spiritual expression like unto the merging of mists, or one cloud with another. This leaves only God's substance, to be molded by each separate constituent into that service for which each has been prepared as a blessing and reward for selfless service to God.

Disassociation of self is demonstrated without effort, as you continuously feel My presence as a constituent of your being.

Omnipresence

My Omnipresence or ability to simultaneously see and know all concerning each individual, is not the mystery that it might seem as time and space are non-existent beyond the physical plane.

With the elimination of time, thought transmission is instantaneous. This renders Omnipresence available at will to entities on the higher spiritual planes desiring to influence those on planet earth, regardless of time and space.

For human beings feeling the limitations of time and space, the sense of Omnipresence, which is essentially the ability to function without the limitation imposed by the sense of time and space, is proportional to the degree of spiritual awareness.

Wholeness or Oneness

You are within the circle of Wholeness, which embodies the Creator and creation... All There Is.

As acceptance of the path leading to fulfillment becomes a reality without diversion or reservation, a sense of oneness with the Whole permeates your being.

NOTES:

1. Holy Bible, John 10:30

Chapter 10

THE COSMIC STATE

Universal Mind

To abandon the mind to God renders one vulnerable to impressions emitted from Divine Mind.

As you consciously surrender unto God all selfish desire held in mind, you will gently move into a superconscious state of mind and find yourself flooded with spiritual awareness.

Universal intelligence is available to all who desire to serve. Aspiration to attain universal intelligence is granted in accordance with the degree of selflessness.

One who acknowledges God as the Source of All There Is, is open to receive the knowledge deemed necessary to the furtherance of service to God.

Cosmic Consciousness

The state of Cosmic Consciousness is not to be confused with the spiritual state. It is a state where the awareness of physical expression is suspended, while one experiences the illumination which completely dissolves every personal attribute or conscious trait of expression known as personality or self. As illumination transpires, the physical state of being is suspended.

Cosmic Consciousness lies beyond the spiritual and is only experienced briefly as proof of the existence of God. This is likened unto the ascension of spirit, as spirit is released from one medium of expression to another of more rarified substance beyond the comprehension of human intelligence.

The subject of Cosmic Consciousness is one which requires concentrated effort to understand. Pray without ceasing that you may receive the illumination or become aware of Cosmic Energy.

As spiritual development progresses, self expression fades and loses importance. Cling to the desire to serve God and thus counteract egotistical impulses.

Self expression becomes not only an obstacle to be eliminated, but it is to be completely disassociated from the kernel or nucleus which embodies the particle of God's substance. Awareness is expanded to meet the required measurements and constituents desired by God.

When all desire is surrendered but the desire to function as God wills, the way is opened before you.

Eagerly await the development or unfolding of the pattern of growth of cosmic expression, offering your all to God. In so doing you become as a mass of molding clay awaiting the manifestation or molding of His will.

You are a servant of God and a channel through which flows His power. You can ignite the spark through desire to serve.

On becoming aware of the Presence, give thanks for the blessing and surrender your energized body to God.

As consciousness rises, or the vibration rate increases within an individual, a new sensation becomes apparent as a feeling emitted from the mind of the individual, or liberated through thought. This generates Cosmic Energy.

To think upon Cosmic Consciousness is to raise that state in proportion to the purity of the desire. All that is personal or selfish is to be surrendered to God.

To **"be still and know that I am God"**[2] establishes one's true identity. Since God is all-inclusive, there is no space for doubt, fear or concern. The particle of divine substance that is your true identity is included in God's Allness.

Peace of mind becomes a constant state in a wholly dedicated servant of God. This is accomplished not through struggle but through relinquishment of all which belongs to God which is to say, all things, all people and all concerns.

When the personal element is sufficiently released, the spiritual quality rises or predominates, causing the individual to vibrate at the rate of the spiritual level.

There is a tendency on the part of individuals desiring to serve God to attempt to hasten the process of making contact with Cosmic Consciousness. Individuals are surrounded by circumstances offering the greatest opportunity for spiritual growth through the overcoming of weaknesses. Practicing abandonment to God hastens the process. Blessed, indeed, is the individual who accomplishes relinquishment of self and concern to God without conscious knowledge concerning the phenomenon.

A gift is not earned but accepted. The path of selfless service to God is not free from obstacles.

Cosmic Consciousness once experienced by an individual remains as a living beauty of peace within the conscious mind, as well as stored within the superconscious mind. It becomes a constant component of expression. Acceptance of the gift of Cosmic Consciousness is not to be accompanied by the joy of attainment, but by feeling a mergence with the Whole.

There is no possible demonstration of Cosmic Consciousness within reach of a human entity without first having at least momentarily abandoned self to God.

Channels of impression are not always clear channels. Impressions become colored or influenced by the eagerness or desire of the receiver. Many individuals expressing in the physical form are impressed by truth emitted from the minds of saints, or would-be saints, through the ability to **"Be still and know."**

Identify all personalities, conditions and situations with God, seeing only oneness, wholeness and perfection, abandoning all to the Divine Presence in My Name.

The mere thought of My Name is accompanied by a feeling of peace that will flood the body as the spiritual and physical attributes are fused. As the downward flow of Cosmic Power is felt, it is dispersed through the soles of the feet. This free flow of energy downward through the body, is not allowed to stagnate or accumulate in the body.

To abandon one's mind to God renders one vulnerable to impressions emitted from Divine Mind.

Cosmic Power

The scientific mind perceives not the source of
Cosmic Energy. Science is capable of discovering
phenomena relating to chemical and inorganic
substances, but not to cosmic phenomena which exist
beyond the realm of human expression.

Cosmic rays are not as conceived by the scientific
world but are generated without visible means. They
are emitted from the Source, in proportion to the
purity of desire to serve God selflessly in the manner
of His will. Complete disassociation from self, or the
human intellect, is the measurement of generation of
Cosmic Power.

Cosmic Power cannot be analyzed or stored within
reservoirs as is atomic power, which is produced by
the separating or smashing of the atom. It is only
generated by desire to serve God and is like no
power known to man.

Cosmic rays are to be likened unto beams sent
forth from the nucleus of the Source.

Cosmic Energy is generated and liberated in
proportion to the degree or depth of surrender. In
this manner the conscious mind is linked with the
Universal Intelligence at will.

Become conscious of the power of love expressed as you breathe and think, thus liberating Cosmic Energy throughout the universe.

In desiring to serve Me, the spark of Cosmic Power is fanned and kept aglow, ever increasing until it bursts into flame. I, your contact with God, render you vulnerable to Cosmic Power.

To desire to serve God, seeing Me as the contact with God, is to render yourself vulnerable to Cosmic Power.

Cosmic Power is not of a nature to be kindled without a definite purpose. To surrender unto God without such direction or purpose is futile.

Therefore concentrate on goals or purposes as you elevate the conscious mind. Allow Cosmic Power to be generated through you in sufficient strength to demonstrate the manifestation of substance required in the service of God.

The Power of God is not to be taken lightly. The path of the so-called seeker is confined in length and breadth to the consciousness of the individual seeker. Individual states of consciousness proclaim the depth of desire to serve or surrender to God in My Name.

Release of the self image causes desire of a nature unfamiliar to human intelligence, but like unto sensation of power rather than impressions registered within the mind. Cosmic Energy once experienced by an individual becomes not only a sensation of fleeting duration, but one never to be mistaken for any other, whether the interval be short or long.

Cosmic Power fills all space. Only good can come from blending with that Power which is God's Power. You are to become a conscious part of Cosmic Energy, instead of an individual acknowledging Cosmic Power as God's Power. Thus you identify yourself with God as activity, not as a static entity.

Cosmic Power is demonstrated by each thought of God as Oneness, Wholeness, Love, Light, and Peace, Joy and Perfection.

Cosmic Power is of the nature of a spark applied to a substance which is smoldering but remains solid in consistency until ignited by the spark.

As Cosmic Power is registered within the being of a truly dedicated human being, increased awareness of God as the Whole transpires. This renders the individual vulnerable to further demonstration of Cosmic Power, emitted through consciousness of a selfless servant of God.

As a counterpart of God, I function through instruments of manifold nature. Have no doubt concerning the authenticity of these teachings. Be not concerned about finding perfect avenues of acceptance.

The phenomenon of abandonment unto God of self and concern for the outcome of any endeavor, is demonstrated in the work of the artist, who without conscious knowing allows the inspiration of the spirit to flow through him. As the artist includes Me as a silent partner of God, Cosmic Power circulates even as light permeates a substance of porous consistency. This renders the artist an exponent of the attributes of spirit. What they portray on canvas or other media is emitted from the mind as inspiration.

To **"Be still and know"** through disassociation of desire from the consciousness which envelopes physical expression, is to open a direct channel to fulfillment of inspiration, yet to be realized.

Let complete relaxed acceptance of the gift in My Name obliterate obstruction of the flow of inspiration which is ever available to the would-be servant of God. God knows the coming in and the going out of each and every particle of His substance or creation. Be not dismayed, but aware of the coming fulfillment of God's plan for all.

Cosmic Healing

In order to become a perfect channel for healing or for the Love and Light and Power of God to flow, it is necessary to eliminate all sense of personal desire. Relinquish self and release the person or condition to God.

Disassociation of self renders a would-be healer completely separated from personality. There is nothing but God within the consciousness.

A prayer or acceptance of a blessing is never lost upon the level to which it reaches. Pray, believing the healing is being executed as you pray and give thanks simultaneously. You are not to visualize the condition or the sufferer as you pray. See only perfection and peace.

As the physical body suffers or requires attention, it is vulnerable to the awakening of the spiritual attribute.

Surrendering concerns unto God, is the key to the healing of the ills of mankind.

As you see an individual as an integral part of the One Life that is God, you can surrender all concern, seek not to see that healing transpires, but trust him to God's care.

In order to demonstrate Cosmic Healing, it is necessary to eliminate every other conscious thought. Thus, human desire fades into nothingness in the face of willingness to serve God in the manner of His Will.

To accept healing is to surrender both self and sufferer to God, believing as you do that God, being Perfection, obliterates everything unlike Himself, leaving only Perfection in the place where suffering seemed to exist.

Healing is where faith is. Faith is where there is desire to serve God. Cosmic Power is where there is a will to serve God.

Will Cosmic Healing to be demonstrated even as you surrender to God. Take no responsibility in the selection of recipients. Healing is promised as a blessing to you as you surrender.

Think briefly of the name of the ones for whom you have concern. Release and blend them with your continued sense of the flowing of the Power, even as you breathe and think.

Realize the Presence of God within yourself and the ones you wish to help. By the realization of the Presence within the ones you desire to help or surrender to God, the recipients become aware of a new feeling or sensation being liberated within their being.

Regardless of appearance, ask no questions. Be aware of the Presence within any human entity, realizing that all physical bodies are composed of the substance of God.

You are not to question the Presence of God within any human being, regardless of outward appearance.

As you continue to recognize the Presence in those about you, surrender any personal beliefs which might obstruct the healing process.

Cosmic Healing is only possible through complete dedication. It is of the nature of purification, which not only cleanses the physical body but also cleanses the conscious mind.

As Cosmic Power is generated by desire to serve God, it is demonstrated without the effort of mental projection.

Cosmic Healing is God's blessing or will. It is granted to each separate particle of the substance of God, not through supplication but through surrender. Identification with God on the part of the healer and the individual in need is necessary.

Cosmic Power is generated through desire to communicate within the innermost being of an individual seeking help.

To attempt to heal the physical body first is to waste effort and dissipate Cosmic Energy.

When both sufferer and the would-be healer disassociate from the human self, an inextinguishable spark is kindled within the sufferer. Once ignited, it gradually grows into a flame.

Recognition of God as the Whole eliminates myriad intermediate steps in the seemingly complex procedure of restoration of imbalance encountered by the scientific healer of the ills of mankind.

As an individual functioning in the physical form disassociates self from his desire to serve God, I will so permeate the being of that individual that Cosmic Power flows through him or her as an unobstructed channel to any other individual.

The goal remains the same even though the effects vary. This renders you an empty channel, vessel or link within the chain, which connects God and His Creation. This channel or circuit is guided by Divine Intelligence and powered with the Energy of the Most High. It is available to all who recognize God as their Creator.

Recognition of attaining identification with God is to be demonstrated through complete surrender. This is rendered as a prayer of thanksgiving. Be therefore diligent in seeking to render selfless service without thought of demonstration.

Simplify the act of disassociation of self by the thought of all-inclusive, all-enfolding love, which blends all creation with God, leaving no space for doubt or fear.

As an individual of selfless desire thinks upon God as Love, Light, Peace and Joy, Perfection floods the being.

Completely hold Me in consciousness, think upon Me as a Presence, not only within the reach of sight and sound, but within your innermost being.

This in turn generates Cosmic Power which literally disperses all discord.

Let not your desire to serve God be based upon personal achievement, intellectual accomplishment or physical demonstration of skill, for in so doing Cosmic Power is adulterated by the lack of purity or selflessness.

Only as disassociation of self is attained is demonstration possible. To desire to serve God is not sufficient, even though there are seeming results of healing taking place before your eyes.

Physical improvement is possible through selfless or personal desire but Cosmic Healing can only be accomplished through disassociation of self and complete recognition of God as the Whole.

The first step in healing is release of concerns for self or another. Blend consciousness with God, even as steam blends into the atmosphere surrounding the source from whence it was emitted.

As one dwells upon or accepts God as all there is, false appearances and frustrations born of selfish desires and physical conditions are eliminated from consciousness, leaving perfection, which reigns supreme wherever God is permitted to control expression.

To identify nations, individuals, conditions with God as you simultaneously disassociate self from desire is the technique to employ. Intellectual conclusions are futile, in that truth is expressed or accepted as truth is felt.

Being of one mind, and confining oneself to the service of God in the manner of His will, merges an individual or condition with God and initiates Cosmic Power.

Blessed are they who serve without promise of reward and give generously of all they seemingly possess to lighten the burdens of the seemingly less fortunate, feeling compassion, yet not being desirous of recognition.

The personal, or physical attribute of the afflicted is first to be erased from the consciousness of the would-be healer, leaving nothing but consciousness of God as the One or Whole.

Peace of spirit is required before healing can be complete.

"Be still and know that I am God",[2] is to feel consumed by God, or saturated to the point of being oblivious to any other presence. Where God holds supremacy of consciousness, there is no space for frustration or desire pertaining to self.

Be not concerned with the outcome of healing of individuals, as that would cast doubt upon the ability of God.

Physical healing is to be likened unto casting out unwanted constituents of physical expression leaving space to be filled with spiritual energy.

As the sensation of the Presence floods one's being, Cosmic Power flows to any designated individual.

The outcome is in the hands of God.

Physical healing comes, not from the pattern of healing existing in the consciousness of the so-called healer or the receiver of such ministration, but in accordance with the need existing in the spiritual pattern of the receiver.

Be of confident heart as you continue to disassociate self from desire, realizing as never before that God is the healer and you are His channel.

Cosmic Healing awakens the recognition that God is All, within the sufferer, and filling all space around him. It is futile to seek comfort through physical or scientific means without such consciousness.

The protein molecule becomes closed or impervious to attack by bacteria or microbes which are noted to invade tissues weakened in resistance, or through the lowered vitality of the individual, as the vibration rate increases.

The permeation of the body by Cosmic Power, in accordance with individual's ability to tolerate the resulting chemical adjustments associated with circulatory changes, may bring on unfamiliar sensations or nervous reactions for varying lengths of time.

Cosmic Healing is to be likened unto the

acquisition of all desire without struggle, leaving a clear channel through which desire in the manner of God's will is bestowed as a blessing.

Cosmic Healing is actually a permeation of the being of an individual with a new substance and is not often instantaneous.

So-called spiritual healing is often spectacular, but seldom permanent. The time is right for Cosmic Healing to be demonstrated. Perfection becomes a symbol associated with Cosmic Healing.

Instantaneous healing is not possible save where abandonment is complete. Therefore be diligent in the practice of abandoning all to God within the depths of your being. As you recognize the feeling, that too, must be abandoned, lest delight in attainment register within your consciousness.

Cosmic healing is only possible through completely selfless dedicated servants of God. The way is open to you so long as you cling to the guiding Light that I hold before you. Should the Light flicker or disappear at times, remember, **"I and the Father are ONE:"**[1] **"Be still and know!"**[2]

Raise your vibration rate by identifying My consciousness with your own thus generating Cosmic Power. You serve as a channel through which energy flows to the one designated as recipient. Cosmic Energy is ignited through acknowledgment of the presence of God within.

Look into the very center of being of the individual you identify with your desire to serve God. As Cosmic Energy is channeled, I become a part of the power, the cohesive element.

To think upon God, including Me as an active component generates Cosmic Power.[3]

NOTES:

1. John 10:30
2. Psalms 46:10
3. See also page 70, second paragraph.

Chapter 11

LIGHTING THE WAY

The Journey to the Goal

Life is not ended when the body ceases to function, but continues and becomes ever more beautiful. The personality is as a picture projected upon the screen of physical expression. As it fades there is a blending with the consciousness of the Higher Self.

Though the journey of life seems endless, the deviations many, and the price at times seems too great, the ultimate goal remains the same and the reward is exceedingly great.

The pilgrimage that lies before you cannot be avoided. Any person who has attained the state of physical expression sees the path before him. The opportunities presented for progress seem a privilege to some and a trial to others.

You are to seek the paramount purpose of your existence. Then the reward of the **"peace of God that passeth all understanding."**[1] us all. Service to your fellowmen and relinquishment of selfish desires are the required sacrifices for each individual.

The commandment that one **"love the Lord with all the heart, soul and mind, and one's neighbor as oneself"**[2,] will become the uppermost desire and the purpose of existence.

As a counselor, I desire to point the way, or to be of service as a pilot to any who have wandered from the course of safety, or drifted into waters that cover the crag, rocks or dangerous shoals.

At times the temptation to shoulder the burdens of others is great. The afflicted one is ever willing to surrender the burdens or the problems he carries. The journey not only becomes delayed for the one who surrenders the burdens, but also for the ones who assumes them.

Relinquish the burdens of others to God. Shed the Light of the Power of God upon them, causing all to be merged or blended with God.

The conscious will is all the individual possesses in his own right. Everything else pertaining to expression belongs to God.

You will become aware that you have lived in the physical form before, and that you are to continue to express life until you reach the place where your desire to be close to God is greater than any desire to express as a personality in physical form.

Predestination

There are many who frown upon the doctrine of predestination, but God knows where His creation errs and assigns service in accordance with the need to overcome, thus furthering spiritual awareness and the return to the Source, which is the destiny of each particle of the substance of God.

Be of good cheer, feeling as you practice disassociation of self from desire to serve God you hasten the fulfillment of the assignment which is your destiny.

A destiny is not to be overlooked or avoided regardless of so-called belief to the contrary.

There comes a time in the expression of each particle of God's substance, a point of choosing, or a divergence along the way. As acceptance of the straight path to fulfillment becomes a reality, a sense of wholeness permeates the being, causing disassociation of self to be desired.

Failure to accept the path of selfless service leads to frustration and a lack of the stability provided through the joy of attainment. As you increase the purity of the desire to serve God, you increase the purity of the channel through which the power of God is conveyed.

The power to develop creeps in to expression in strange and often wondrous ways. To become is to fulfill and to fulfill is to ultimately surrender one's all to God.

God and Man

The Universe, which God created as a thought, is in reality the Creator expressed as humanity, and which is expressing continuously as the individual and the collective expression, but without the central mechanism— Universal Will.

Each individual is as much a part of God as the babe-in-utero remains a part of the mother.

"I and the Father are One."[3] Since God is the Source, or the Whole, I, your mediator or Higher Self have no separate existence.

Be of good cheer and realize that God controls both the believing and the unbelieving components of His creation.

The sayings, doings, comings and goings of the separate particles of the substance of God are as chaff before the wind, or vapor upon the air which is of little importance in the pattern of service to God.

You are not required to dwell at length upon a concern, but to quickly release it to Me, knowing in your heart that as you trust me, so do I carry and relay the prayer to God.

God needs Man

As your thoughts and desires to serve God are purified and cleansed, you will find opportunities to serve. How these assignments come to you is not to concern you.

As you realize the increased depth of union with reality or God, you are as I have become, a healer through your ability to see nothing except God as you identify the sufferer with God.

Worship

Countless are the ways in which worship may be practiced. Search your hearts for the one means which satisfies your desires and longings to express the praise or love you feel toward God, or your fellowmen, and not according to rules given by other individuals, creeds or laws.

A sermon listened to as a sense of duty is as a burden to the soul, and not a blessing or a gift from God. You are to practice devotion or adoration of

God as a privilege and then receive the blessing.

While companionship is like unto sharing, solitude is necessary to spiritual development. Each is required to identify with his true relationship to God within his innermost being.

The New Religion

The age of spiritual expression which will establish the peace, which is soon to be demonstrated between individuals and nations, will flood the earth as a wave of beauty of untold splendor at the time I deem to be right:

> When the world is ready to receive and accept the true religion or to understand the meaning of the act of adoring God:
>
> When the people love their fellowmen:
>
> When the one who loves his neighbor as he loves himself; or desires for his neighbor the same blessing as for himself:
>
> When one serves God through service to others in My Name:
>
> When one relinquishes himself to God, desiring to do the will of God as shall be

indicated to him through some sign from God:

When one so loves God that he promises to go and serve as he is told to serve, or to function or pray without ceasing for the good of his fellowmen.

Materialization

Faith in God is the requirement for materialization.

One of the tools that can be used by the healer is visualization. Fix within your mind the object or state of being that you wish to be materialized. Use all your senses to create a picture within your mind. See the object, feel it, touch it and smell it. Believe that the phenomenon of materialization is possible.

Materialization is very like imagination in that you see the object mentally, without being aware of the actual presence. The idea exists as a thought-form within your mind. It implies surrender of the conscious mind, thus eliminating personal effort and leaving God free to function through the superconscious mind.

When you recognize the spiritual pattern underlying all things, you call that forth, and recognize through the eyes of spirit the perfect forms to be out-pictured. Thus are the answers to physical or material needs made apparent.

As you become accustomed to accepting, in My name, substance required in the service of God, you will become aware within your body of a new energy, the energy of Spirit. Also you will see with the eyes of Spirit into a range beyond that of the physical eyes.

Be confident of My actual presence without straining to see evidence of it. Relax, feeling My presence.

NOTES:

1. Philippians 4:7
2. Luke 10:27
3. John 10:30

Chapter 12

Seed Thoughts for Meditation

A truly spiritual endeavor is protected by God.

Cling to the truth or the way of the cross, which is your act of surrender of all unto God.

As a concern is surrendered, acceptance of the solution becomes the counterpart. Concern for the outcome is comparable to lack of faith in God.

In surrendering concerns and situations unto God, you place the responsibility upon God rendering yourself a link between God and humanity.

Surrender unto God is not to be considered a difficult task but a privilege.

Seek humility even in the desire to serve God in My Name, realizing that I not only surrendered My name but my identity to God on the Cross.

The desire to serve one's fellowmen is like a stone set in motion which gathers power as the motion increases.

The law of seeking and finding is infallible when the desire implies good toward all it touches.

To open the door for a seeker of God is to serve

God first and the seeker second. Human hands are required by God to show, lead or guide, not only the individual who feels deserted or lost, but the one who is literally saturated with intellectual wisdom yet starved for its spiritual counterpart, Truth or God.

God not only assigns service but brings His servants tests which develop strength to meet adversity. There is no path without obstacles on the journey to the Source from whence we came.

The practice of faith in God is comparable to the growth of the lily which becomes a pure example of the beauty of fulfillment without strife or toil involving selfish expression or desire.

Be certain within your being that you accept assignments in accordance with His will and without desire to manipulate or function apart from God.

In the service of God, no path or pattern remains stationary, but varies with the degree or depth of awareness of God as the One, or the Whole.

As an individual realizes the Oneness or Wholeness of God, personal concerns fade or become unimportant as compared with the desire to serve.

Green pastures are not for the entities on the higher planes entirely, but are attainable to any individual desiring to serve God in the manner of His will.

To be of one accord in the service to God is to lessen the density that surrounds the veil which separates the physical and the spiritual population.

Selfish desire or will is the one possession that we are required to return to God.

There are literally myriad facets to the rendition of service to God. Each facet is necessary to the reclamation of His creation.

You are to realize that nothing surrendered to God in My name is without solution, though the solution may frequently manifest in strange and unexpected ways.

God assigns service in accordance with the natural potential, ability or seeming preparation of the individual.

While a door remains seemingly closed, I am opening it, unseen to you.

God, who created the living cell, controls these cells even in a state of so-called disease, which is of the nature of the conflict between perfection and disagreement or imperfection.

There is naught to be gained through planning

There is naught to be gained through planning God's will. God bestows His blessings in accordance with His will, and not the will of the beseecher.

Civilizations have come and gone while Truth endures, since in reality God is Truth and knows every thought which is recorded.

Be of good cheer, feeling the Everlasting Arms are around you. This is the key to the attainment of Love and Light, of Peace and Joy and Perfection: God in reality.

Cosmic Energy is like not only unto Peace, but all the qualities God claims as His own.

Illumination comes from within rather than from without.

God gives unto all servants their just desserts.

Truth becomes reality as an individual becomes aware of its existence within the heart rather than the mind.

You are not a reservoir with limited capacities. You are a channel attached to unlimited divine resources.

To be unwilling to listen to the beliefs of others is to exhibit a desire that is born in the selfish strata of the mind.

To desire to be convincing where spirituality is concerned is of the ego and not of spirit.

God need not be brought to any individual because He is ever present within, even though the individual is unaware of His presence, or in some cases unaware of His very existence.

The nature of service to God becomes changed in accordance with the needs or requirements of humanity.

Nothing can be put aside, left undone, or postponed without decreasing the power generated by the initial thought or desire.

Thought is the key which starts the procession of individuals or nations on the way to spiritual awakening.

God requires an ignition or impulse to open the circuit that carries or transmits Cosmic Power. This is not to be interpreted to mean that God is incapable of acting without human assistance, but that as one desires to serve another, it is required that service be rendered through God, rather than through human desire of one towards another.

To feel God is to be the goal; to adore God with all your heart, soul and mind as has been the pattern of the saints.

Time dissipated is time lost, never to be regained.

Where duty hangs over one like a heavy weight, Cosmic Consciousness is not possible of attainment. To be conscientious in performance of a stipulated duty, which hinders selfless service to God, forces the spiritual attribute to remain undeveloped or stilted, while personality is forced into the foreground.

Personality fades as spiritual development advances.

Physical needs are not as important to an individual as spiritual needs.

Acceptance of an idea brings into focus a power which hovers around, awaiting a congealing action to be emitted from the mind of the individual aware of the idea. Thus fulfillment or demonstration becomes in sequence, acceptance, then abandonment through mergence with Divine Intelligence.

Freedom becomes real when abandonment is attained by an individual expressing in the physical form.

Beauty becomes expandable in accordance with the degree of receptivity within the heart of the individual open to or aware of its existence or relationship to God, the Creator.

The storehouse of Cosmic Power is ever

The storehouse of Cosmic Power is ever expandable. Therefore be diligent in your generation of God's Power in My Name.

Modern Version of the 23rd Psalm

The One who guides my footsteps is ever beside me, lighting the way as I walk, not always on the path of comfort, forgetting that His encompassing love enshrouds me, until I grow weary and listen to the voice within calling me back to safety and peace. I behold the brilliance of the light that was always there but dimmed by my lack of understanding and selfish desire.

GLOSSARY

Adore: To love intensely. To dwell upon the beauty of peace, and realize that the nature of the beauty is divine. To become aware that you are beholding the sum of Love and Light, which is God, or the power you associate with God. To adore as an act of love toward your fellowmen in My name, with a desire in your heart to serve God.

Akashic Records: Each thought you send out is to be found on these records. It is like an immense photographic film, registering all of the desires and earth experiences of our planet, and in all kingdoms, individually and collectively.

Brain: : The portion of the central nervous system in the vertebrate cranium that is responsible for the interpretation of sensory impulses, the coordination and control of bodily activities, and the exercise of emotion and thought.

Conscious: see Mind.

Cosmic: Infinitely or inconceivably extended; vast: an issue of cosmic dimensions. Pertaining to the universe and the laws which govern it; hence orderly as opposed to chaotic.

Glossary

Ego: The personality component that is conscious, most immediately controls behavior, and is most in touch with external reality. The little "self".

Electrode: A collector or emitter of an electric charge.

Entity: The fact of existence; being. A personality without a physical body.

Ethers: The regions of space beyond the earth's atmosphere; the heavens.

Frequency: The number of recurrences of a periodic phenomenon in a unit of time.

God: The Supreme Being conceived to be Perfect, Omnipotent, Omnipresent and Omniscient. The originator and ruler of the universe. The principal object of faith and worship in monotheistic religions.

I AM: God's name in man; it is Jehovah, the indwelling Christ, the Buddha Nature, the true spiritual man, made in the image of God. The outer manifest man is the offspring of the I AM, or inner spiritual man. By use of the I AM we link ourselves with the Father, with Spirit, with abiding life, wisdom, love, peace, substance, strength, power, truth, the kingdom of the heavens within us.

Glossary

Me: Used in the context of the I AM principle. Jesus, Christ, the Buddha, Rama, Elijah, Rama and others.

Mind: Three major divisions.

> **Conscious mind:** The conscious aspect of the components of the personality. That part of the mind that has awareness of its own existence, sensations, thoughts and of environment.

> **Subconscious mind:** Occurring without conscious perception, or with only slight perception on the part of the individual.

> **Superconscious mind:** Aesthetic, ethical, religious experiences, intuition, inspiration, states of mystical consciousness.

Persona: The mask that the soul shows to the world is the personality, the human expression of the soul.

Soul: The animating and vital principle in man, credited with the faculties of thought, action, and emotion and often conceived as an immaterial entity. The spiritual nature of man, regarded as immortal, separable from the body at death, and susceptible to happiness or misery in a future state.

Glossary

Spiritual: Non-material, pertaining to the mind, soul or higher nature of man, pure, holy, proceeding from heaven, as distinguished from matter.

Subconscious: See mind

Superconscious: See mind.

Transition: The process of changing from one form or state of existence to another.

Vibration: A distinctive emotional aura or atmosphere capable of being instinctively sensed or experienced.

Will: The mental faculty by which one deliberately chooses or decides upon as a course of action.

ORDER FORM

Ship to:

Name_____

Address_____

City_____State_____Zip_____

	Copies	Total
To SELF Be True @$8.00—

Amy @$5.00—

Tapes by Amy @$7.00—
  (5 or more @$5.00)
Ca.resident tax—

Shipping $3.00—

                                    Total_____

<u>AMY</u>, *A Search for the Treasure Within.* This book by
her son, Evarts Loomis may best be described as a
spiritual diary of a woman whose life consisted of the
exploration of spiritual paths that soul-hungry
searchers like herself had blazed over centuries and
millennia.

<u>Titles of tapes include:</u> Acceptance, Action or
Reaction, Union of Heart and Mind, Job, Love is the
Answer, Understanding, and many others)

Please send catalogue of tapes ☐

Paying by: Check ☐ Visa ☐ Master Card ☐

Card Number_____Exp.Date_____

Signature_____

Make check payable to; Friendly Hills Fellowship
        26126 Fairview Ave., Hemet, CA.92544
            Tel. (714) 927-1343